PLAY LIKE A GIRL

VOLLEYBALL

BY

EMILIE DUFRESNE

KidHaven PUBLISHING

Published in 2020 by
KidHaven Publishing, an Imprint of Greenhaven Publishing, LLC
353 3rd Avenue
Suite 255
New York, NY 10010

Edited by: Robin Twiddy
Designed by: Danielle Jones

Cataloging-in-Publication Data

Names: Dufresne, Emilie.
Title: Volleyball / Emilie Dufresne.
Description: New York : KidHaven Publishing, 2020. | Series: Play
like a girl | Includes glossary and index.
Identifiers: ISBN 9781534531017 (pbk.) | ISBN 9781534530102
(library bound) | ISBN 9781534531338 (6 pack) | ISBN
9781534530959 (ebook)
Subjects: LCSH: Volleyball--Juvenile literature.
Classification: LCC GV1015.34 D847 2020 | DDC 796.325--dc23

Printed in the United States of America

CPSIA compliance information: Batch #BS19KL: For further information contact Greenhaven
Publishing LLC, New York, New York at 1-844-317-7404.

Please visit our website, www.greenhavenpublishing.com.
For a free color catalog of all our high-quality books, call toll free
1-844-317-7404 or fax 1-844-317-7405.

IMAGE CREDITS

Cover - Andrey_Popov, supparsorn, NPaveIN, Photo Melon, margostock, alarich, BigMouse, MyImages - Micha. 3 - Andrey_Popov. 4 - A_Lesik, Roka
Pics. 5 - muzsy, Roka Pics. 6 - Halfpoint, Avatar_023, MilanTomazin. 7 - Roman Samborskyi, kubais, Pukhov K. 8&9 - Igor Kovalchuk, hystovskaya
katsiaryna, Zilu8, Syda Productions, stockyimages, Vagengeim. 10 - ostill, Aspen Photo. 11 - ostill, muzsy. 12 - Paolo Bona. 13 - Stuart Monk.
14 - margostock, Paolo Bona. 15 - Tomasz Trojanowski, ilusmedical. 16 - titov dmitriy, dotshock. 17 - ESB Professional, Paolo Bona.
18 - enterlinedesign. 19 - Boris Ryaposov, dotshock. 20 - Boris Ryaposov, dotshock. 21 - muzsy, antoni halim, Feng Yu. 22 - wavebreakmedia
A_Lesik. 23 - Paolo Bona, Alexey V Smirnov, CP DC Press. 24 - CP DC Press, mooinblack. 25 - Chatchai Somwat, mooinblack. 26 - Mascha Tace,
CE Photography. 27 - STILLFX. 28 - Helder Almeida, Kamira, Roka Pics. 29 - monticello, Boris Ryaposov, Sergey Novikov, ImageFlow. 30 - Monkey
Business Images, AlexLMX, icestylecg. Illustrations by Danielle Jones. Images are courtesy of Shutterstock.com. With thanks to Getty Images,
Thinkstock Photo and iStockphoto.

CONTENTS

Words that look like <u>this</u> are volleyball lingo. Learn more about them on page 8.

Words that look like THIS are explained in the glossary on page 31.

THE BASICS

TEAM HUDDLE

So, you want to play volleyball? This book will teach you all about what to say, what to wear, and how to play. From learning the lingo to earning a place in the Hall of Fame, this book will give you the know-how!

Volleyball has been an official sport of the Summer Olympic Games since 1964.

GRAB YOUR FRIENDS AND YOUR KNEE PADS – IT'S TIME TO PLAY!

Volleyball is a game played by two teams of six players. Each team uses their hands to hit and push the ball over the net onto the other team's side so that it bounces on the ground within the lines on the OPPOSING team's side.

Volleyball is a fast-paced game of rebound. What does rebound mean? Well, in volleyball you can't catch and then throw the ball. Instead you have to bounce the ball off different parts of your arms and hands in order to pass and score.

THE "VOLLEY" IN VOLLEYBALL ALSO MEANS HITTING THE BALL BEFORE IT BOUNCES.

Volleyball may not be a CONTACT SPORT, but the game includes a lot of jumping, sprinting, and diving onto the ground in order to stop the ball from hitting the floor on your side of the court. It is important to wear knee pads and sensible shoes. This sport can leave you a bit bruised!

THE TYPES

BEACH VOLLEYBALL

Beach volleyball is the most commonly played ADAPTATION of indoor volleyball. The biggest difference between the two is that one is played on a solid floor, and the other on sand. Beach volleyball teams only have two players instead of six, and the court is slightly smaller.

NEXT TIME YOU'RE AT THE BEACH, OR NEAR SOME SAND, WHY NOT GIVE IT A TRY?

SNOW VOLLEYBALL

Snow volleyball has similar rules to beach volleyball, except it's slightly colder! Recently, it has become more popular and the FIVB is trying to make it a Winter Olympic sport.

CLEATS

DON'T FORGET TO WEAR CLEATS WHEN PLAYING SNOW VOLLEYBALL SO YOU DON'T SLIP AND FALL!

SITTING VOLLEYBALL

Sitting volleyball is an adaptation of the indoor sport that was originally made for people with disabilities in their lower bodies; it can be played by anyone as long as they follow the rules. The rules are very similar to standing volleyball except that, at all times, a player's rear must be in contact with the floor.

UNOFFICIAL VARIATIONS

As well as these variations, there are some unofficial variations of volleyball. Some examples include aquatic volleyball, in which the players play standing up in the water, nine-a-side volleyball, which has nine players on a team instead of six, and footvolley, which is a mixture of soccer and volleyball.

THE LINGO

The lingo, the slang, the vocab. Whatever you call it, learning the words behind specific sports can be a very daunting task! Here are some of the terms and weirder words that will help you talk the volleyball talk in no time.

GROUNDED
When the ball hits the ground and scores a point.

BUMP
A type of pass where you hold your arms out in front of you, make a fist with one hand, and wrap your other hand around it. You can hit the ball in an upward direction using your forearms.

DIGS
When a ball falls below a player's waist so they either bend or dive lower to the ground in order to stop the opposing team from gaining a point.

BLOCKS
A shot used to stop an attacking shot.

SPIKES

When a player jumps high in the air and hits the ball over the net by hitting it hard and in a downward direction to try to score a point for their team.

ILLEGAL

An action that is not allowed within the rules of volleyball, also known as a violation.

OUT

When the ball goes outside the marked lines of the court.

CARRY

Holding the ball instead of bouncing it off your body. This is against the rules.

SIDE-OUT

When it is the other team's serve but your team wins the point. Your team then has to rotate one position clockwise.

THE PLAYERS

SETTER

The setter's job is to set up the hitter's attacking shots. They often get the second touch of the ball, which is called the "set." Setters try to push the ball high into the air. They do this by holding their hands above their head and pushing the ball into the air using their fingertips.

SETTERS CAN STAND IN ANY POSITION ON THE COURT. PLAYERS MIGHT PREFER A PARTICULAR SIDE DEPENDING ON THEIR DOMINANT HAND.

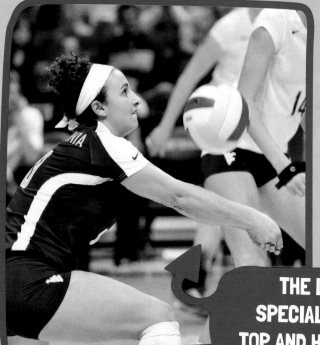

LIBERO

The libero's role is to attempt daring dives and lunges to stop the opposing team from scoring points. They usually stand in the middle of the back row and aren't allowed past the attack line and into the front zone. They also aren't allowed to attack if the ball is above a certain point.

THE LIBERO IS ALSO KNOWN AS A DEFENSE SPECIALIST. THEY WEAR A DIFFERENT-COLORED TOP AND HAVE DIFFERENT RULES COMPARED TO THE OTHER PLAYERS.

HITTERS

Mostly, hitters stand on the front row, close to the net. A hitter could also stand on the back row to help with those tricky shots! It is the hitter's job to hit the ball over the net and score points by hitting <u>spikes</u>. They have to think quickly and be even quicker on their feet in order to score points.

HITTERS HAVE TO BE VERY GOOD AT SEEING WHERE THE SETTERS ARE PASSING THE BALL AND WHERE IT'S BEST TO AIM THE BALL ON THE OPPONENTS' SIDE.

BLOCKERS

Blockers and hitters are the same players that have multiple roles. As well as trying to win points by spiking the ball, they also have to stop the hitters on the opposing team from scoring against them by using <u>blocks</u>. This means jumping as high as they can in the air and putting their hands up to try to stop the ball from entering their side of the court.

THIS CAN BE HARD BECAUSE PLAYERS AREN'T ALLOWED TO TOUCH THE NET!

Find out more about the rules of volleyball on page 20.

ROTATIONS

So now you know what each player does and where they stand, right? Well, not quite. Volleyball isn't that simple. In volleyball, players have to rotate clockwise when they <u>side-out</u>. When you side-out, your team has to rotate one position clockwise.

THE POSITION EACH PLAYER STARTS IN IS THEIR OPTIMUM POSITION. THIS IS THE PLACE WHERE EACH PLAYER IS BEST SUITED.

OPTIMUM POSITIONS

There are six different positions you can be in and they are positioned and numbered like this. These are the best positions that each player can be in.

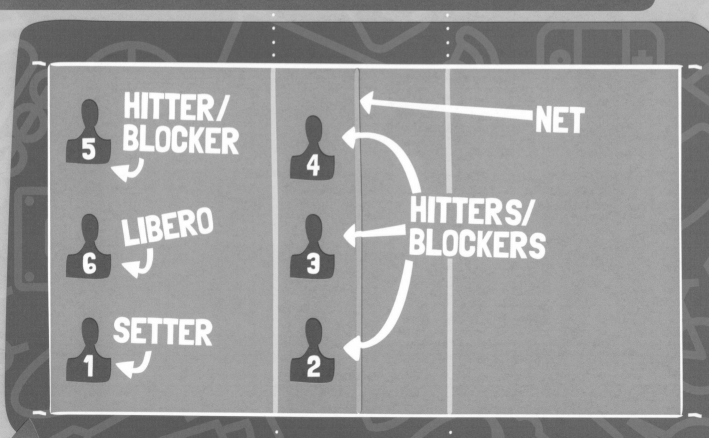

HITTER/BLOCKER
5

LIBERO
6

SETTER
1

NET

4

HITTERS/BLOCKERS

3

2

However, when you side-out, you have to move out of these optimum positions and to a place that might not suit your strengths as well. After you side-out once, you will be in these positions.

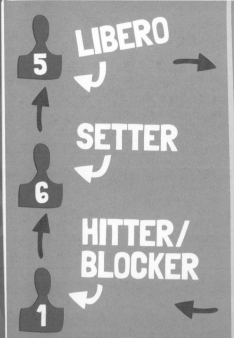

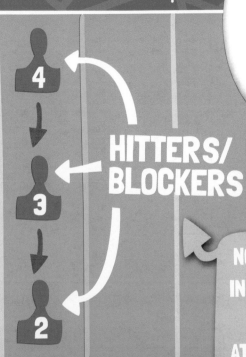

LIBERO

SETTER

HITTER/ BLOCKER

HITTERS/ BLOCKERS

As the libero isn't allowed on the front row, they only rotate between positions 1, 2, and 3.

NOW, THE LIBERO IS NOT IN THE MIDDLE AND CAN'T BLOCK SPIKES THAT ATTACK THE RIGHT-HAND SIDE VERY EASILY.

SUBSTITUTIONS

Because volleyball players are constantly moving into positions that don't best suit their skills, they are allowed to make lots of SUBSTITUTIONS. The FIVB allows a team to make six substitutions per game. This means that if a player is not in the best position for their skill sets, you can swap them for a player that is better suited to that position.

SUBSTITUTE WAITING TO GO ONTO THE COURT

THE UNIFORM

Volleyball is a fast-paced sport that is a very good form of exercise. It is both a form of CARDIO and MUSCLE STRENGTHENING and is great for your physical health. All of this exercise needs the right type of clothing. If you are just playing for fun, make sure you wear something that is comfortable, stretchy, and BREATHABLE.

OFFICIAL UNIFORM

When you play as part of a team for your school or community or even a PROFESSIONAL team, there are certain things you should wear. One of these things is a jersey, or a top. These jerseys are usually tight-fitting and made out of stretchy fabric. You can choose different styles of jersey depending on your PREFERENCES. For example, you could choose to wear sleeves so that your arms are protected from hitting the ball.

VOLLEYBALL ARM-PROTECTOR SLEEVES

On the bottom, volleyball players usually wear bike-style shorts. These give the players lots of flexibility and the ability to move quickly. This is essential for being able to make those daring lunges and <u>digs</u>.

It is also important to wear sensible shoes. When playing indoor volleyball, it is important to wear shoes that provide you with a lot of grip so that you don't slide all over the court when jumping, running, and diving for the ball.

JERSEY TOP

SHORTS

KNEE PADS

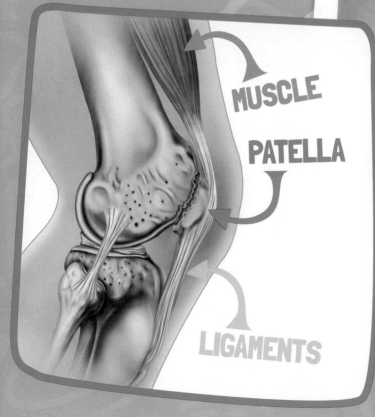

MUSCLE

PATELLA

LIGAMENTS

SNEAKERS

You also need to wear knee pads when playing volleyball. These protect your knees when you fall on the hard surface of the court. They do this by supporting the patella (the kneecap) and the muscles and LIGAMENTS around it. Knee pads also help players perform better, because they don't have to be scared about diving to the ground when making daring digs!

THE EQUIPMENT

THE BALL

Volleyballs are a standardized object within the game. This means there are rules saying what size and weight the ball can be. The average weight of a volleyball is around 9 ounces (250 g).

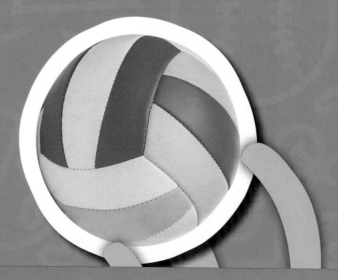

The balls are made up of panels of fabric sewn together in a ball shape. Depending on the weight of a ball, it could travel differently in the air. For example, lighter balls would stay in the air longer, whereas heavier balls would fall to the ground quicker.

THIS IS WHY IT IS IMPORTANT THAT THE BALL IS THE SAME SIZE AND WEIGHT IN EVERY GAME.

In sports, standardized objects make sure that the game is fair, by making sure every game is played with the same type of equipment every time.

THE NET

The net and how high it is hung is also standardized in volleyball. In women's volleyball, the net is hung 7.35 feet (2.24 m) high. For children 10 years old and under, the net is 6.5 feet (1.98 m) high. For 11- and 12-year-olds, it is 7 feet (2.13 m) tall, and for 13- and 14-year-olds, it is around 7.4 feet (2.25 m) high.

THE COURT

The court also has specific measurements and areas. The court is 59 feet (18 m) long and 29.5 feet (9 m) wide. Each team plays in a square that is 29.5 feet (9 m) on every side. Each team's side is split into two areas: the front zone and the back zone. The front zone extends 9.8 feet (3 m) from the net, and only certain positions are allowed to try to win points by spiking from inside this area.

TURN THE PAGE TO SEE HOW BIG THE COURT IS AND HOW IT IS LAID OUT.

THE COURT

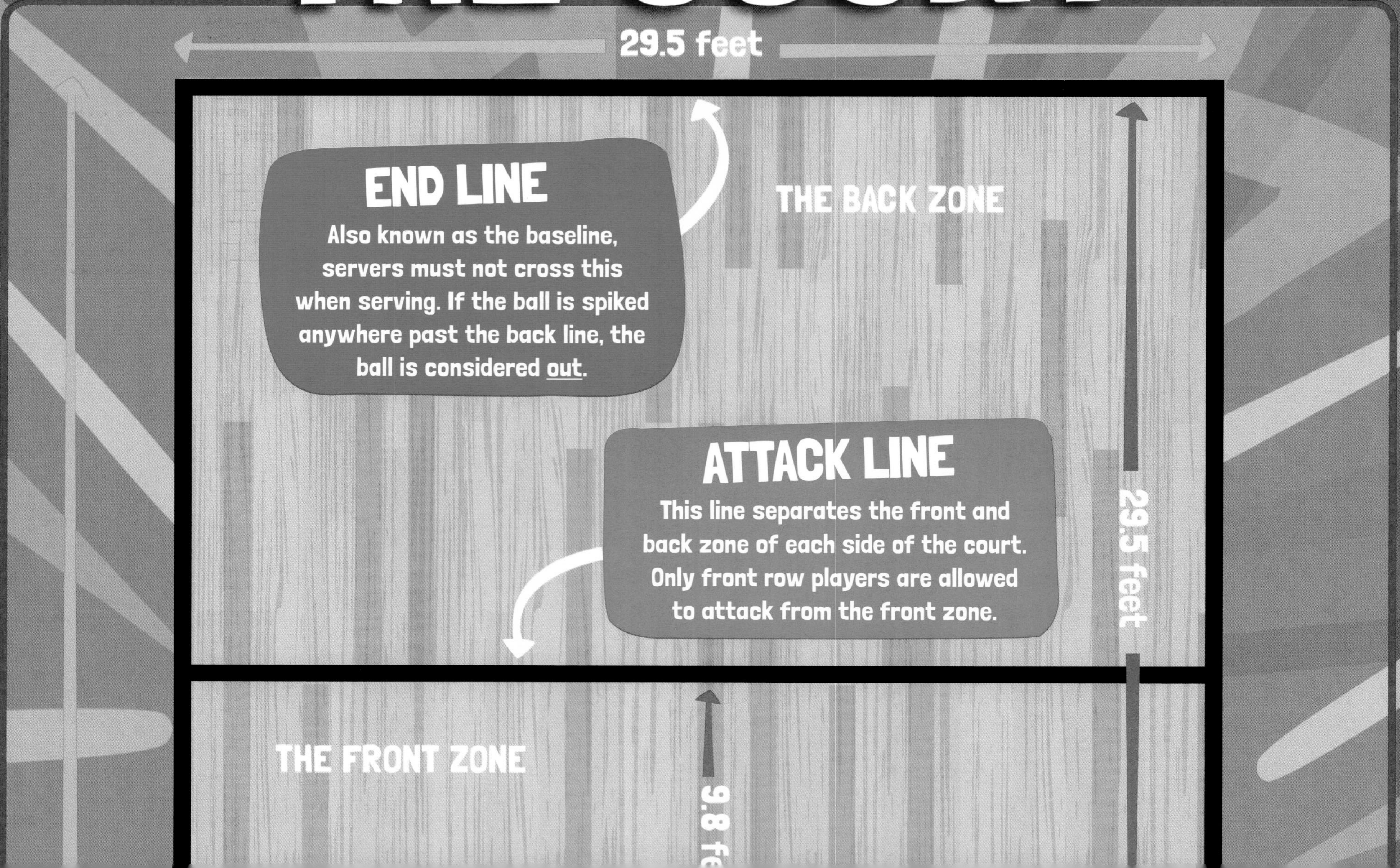

29.5 feet

29.5 feet

9.8 fe

THE BACK ZONE

THE FRONT ZONE

ATTACK LINE

This line separates the front and back zone of each side of the court. Only front row players are allowed to attack from the front zone.

END LINE

Also known as the baseline, servers must not cross this when serving. If the ball is spiked anywhere past the back line, the ball is considered out.

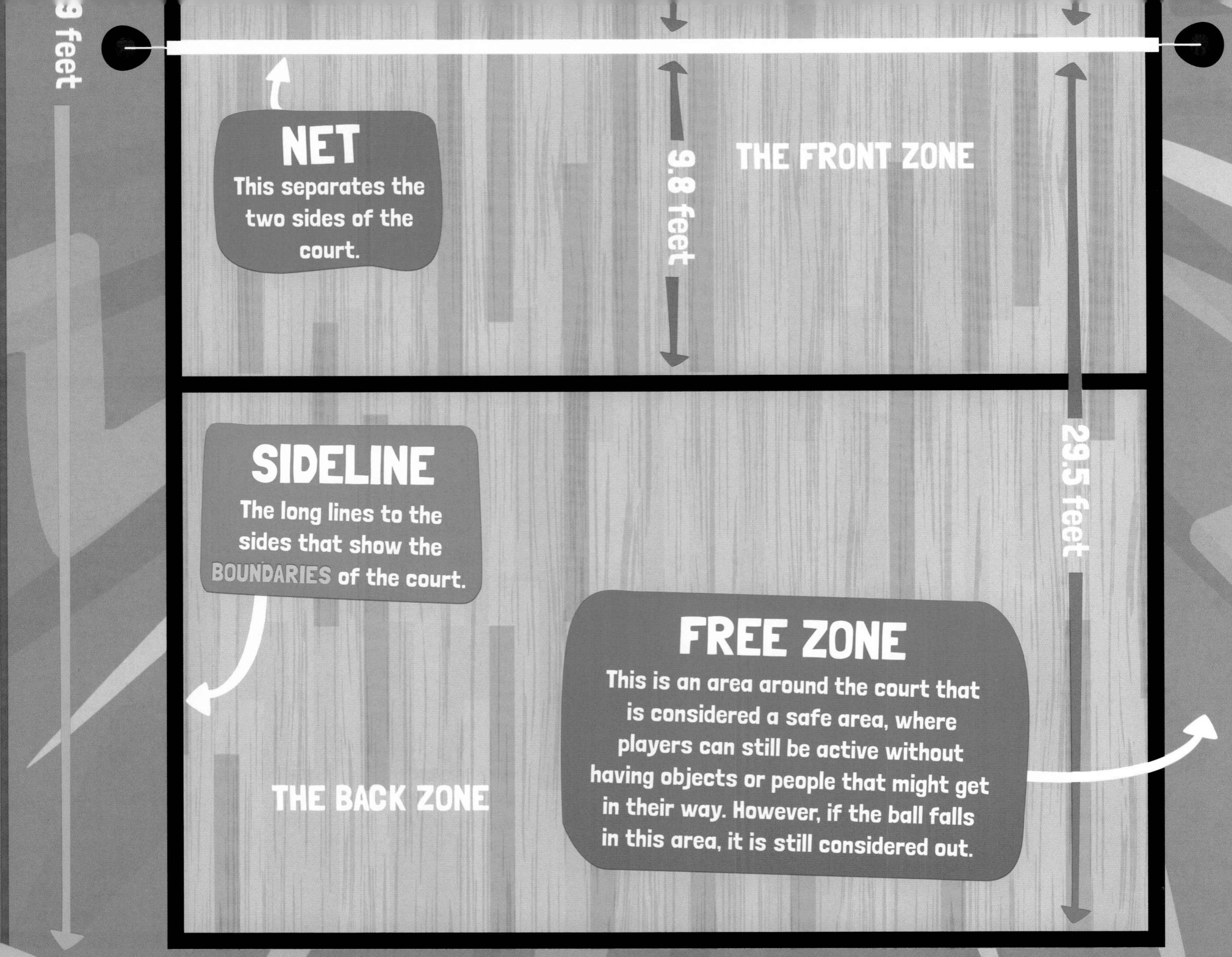

29.5 feet

THE FRONT ZONE

9.8 feet

FREE ZONE

This is an area around the court that is considered a safe area, where players can still be active without having objects or people that might get in their way. However, if the ball falls in this area, it is still considered out.

NET

This separates the two sides of the court.

SIDELINE

The long lines to the sides that show the BOUNDARIES of the court.

THE BACK ZONE

9 feet

THE RULES

BUMP PASS

SERVING

- The server must serve from behind the end line

- The ball can be served overhand or underhand

- The serve must be returned by a <u>bump</u> only

PLAYING

- Each side can only touch the ball three times before hitting it back to the other side

- One player cannot hit the ball twice in a row

- If the ball touches a boundary line, it is considered in

- The ball should not "rest" in your hands (catching, holding, or throwing the ball)

- Serves cannot be blocked or used to attack

- Only the three players in the front row can spike the ball from the front zone

IF YOU CATCH THE BALL INSTEAD OF PASSING IT, IT IS CALLED A <u>carry</u> AND IS AN <u>illegal</u> MOVE.

ILLEGAL MOVES AND VIOLATIONS

- Carrying, holding, or throwing the ball

- Touching the net with any part of your body

- Making an attack from the front zone when you are in a back row position

- When the same player touches the ball twice or more in a row

VOLLEYBALL REFEREE

IF YOU MAKE AN ILLEGAL MOVE OR VIOLATION, A POINT IS GIVEN TO THE OPPOSING TEAM.

15 10 9

KEEPING SCORE

- 1 point is awarded when the ball is <u>grounded</u> within the boundaries of your opponents' court

- 1 point will be awarded to the opposing team if a violation is made

- The first team to score 25 points and be at least two points ahead of the opposing team wins a set

- Up to five sets are played, with the fifth set being a tiebreaker if both teams have won two sets

- The fifth set is only played up to 15 points

- In the fifth set, the team that reaches 15 points first and is at least two points ahead of the other team wins the match

21

THE EVENTS

RECREATIONAL AND REGIONAL TEAMS

If you have a school team or a team that plays RECREATIONALLY and you want to start competing, there are lots of ways you can get involved. Ask a teacher, parent, or sports coach how to join a local league. If you want to take your team further, you could always search for regional teams and see how you get to play for your county or state.

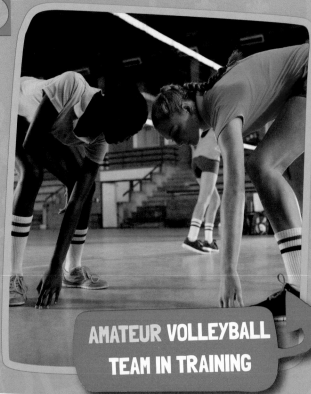

AMATEUR VOLLEYBALL TEAM IN TRAINING

THE BIG LEAGUES

As volleyball players get better and better, they can start playing at higher levels. After regional games come national ones. This means you play teams from all over your country. Then comes playing internationally, which means playing for your country. There are lots of tournaments for different countries and continents around the world, such as the Asian Games, the European Games, the Pan-American Games, the Lusophony Games, and the All-Africa Games.

WORLD TOURNAMENTS

There are many international volleyball competitions in which countries from all over the world compete against each other. Some of these include the World Championships, the World Cup, and the Nations League, which only started in 2018.

ITALIAN FANS CHEERING ON THEIR NATIONAL TEAM AT THE 2014 VOLLEYBALL WORLD CUP

THE OLYMPICS

One of the most PRESTIGIOUS tournaments in the world is the Olympics. Lots of countries compete in a variety of games, one of which is volleyball. Since volleyball became an official Olympic sport in 1964, the team that has won the most gold medals is the Soviet Union, now Russia, with a total of four wins.

RUSSIA, IN BLUE, PLAYING BRAZIL IN THE 2016 OLYMPIC GAMES IN RIO DE JANEIRO

THE ONES TO WATCH

There are some very talented female volleyball players to look out for. Let's find out some more about them.

ZHU TING

FACT FILE:

Date of Birth:
November 29, 1994

Country of Birth:
China

Height:
6'6" (1.98 m)

Position:
Hitter & Captain

Zhu Ting is one of the best volleyball players in the world. At a young age, she already towered over other volleyball players, not just in height, but in achievement. She has won four gold medals and has been named the "Most Valuable Player" many times for lots of different tournaments!

KELLY MURPHY

FACT FILE:

Date of Birth:
October 20, 1989

Country of Birth:
USA

Height:
6'2" (1.88 m)

Position:
Setter & Spiker

After beginning to play volleyball at the age of 11, Kelly Murphy has become a great American volleyball player. She is a member of the United States national team that won a bronze medal in the 2016 Olympics. She has also won a total of four medals while playing for the United States.

PLAY LIKE A GIRL

FABIANA CLAUDINO

FACT FILE:

Date of Birth:
January 24, 1985

Country of Birth:
Brazil

Height:
6'4" (1.93 m)

Position:
Middle Blocker & Captain

Claudino is a Brazilian volleyball player and a blindingly brilliant blocker. Not only did she captain the Brazilian national team to a gold medal in the 2012 Olympics, but since 2006 she has been awarded seven "Best Blocker" awards. No one could block this player from getting to the top!

RACHAEL ADAMS

FACT FILE:

Date of Birth:
June 3, 1990

Country of Birth:
USA

Height:
6'2" (1.88 m)

Position:
Middle Blocker

Rachael Adams helped her team win bronze in the 2016 Olympic Games in Rio. She has won three gold medals while playing for the U.S. in different competitions. She has also been awarded "Best Middle Blocker" twice since 2016.

THE HALL

Even though volleyball isn't the oldest sport, it still has a long history of great female players. Let's take a look at some of the best of the best.

Lang Ping is a former volleyball player and current volleyball coach. Ping was at the top of her game in the 1980s and, as a player, helped win four gold medals for her team. Later in life, she became a coach and even coached the Chinese national team to Olympic gold in 2016. She also became the first volleyball player ever to win gold both as a player and a coach.

Martine Wright is a sitting volleyball player. She lost both her legs in the London bombings of 2005, but went on to play for Great Britain in the London 2012 Paralympics. She continues to be an ambassador for disabled sports and inspires both women and people with disabilities to play sports.

OF FAME

Regla Torres began playing for Cuba in her youth. She was quickly recognized as an up-and-coming star of the sport. As soon as she was old enough, she began playing for the adult team. In 1992, she became the youngest volleyball player to win an Olympic gold medal. She went on to win two more Olympic gold medals with the Cuban team in 1996 and 2000. In 2001, she was awarded the highly prestigious award: "Best Volleyball Player of the Century."

Doaa Elghobashy was part of the first-ever Egyptian team to compete in a beach volleyball tournament at the Olympics. She was also the first woman to wear a hijab at a beach volleyball game in the Olympics.

SHE INSPIRES WOMEN ACROSS THE WORLD TO PLAY WHATEVER SPORT THEY WANT TO, NO MATTER WHERE THEY ARE FROM OR WHAT THEY WEAR – AND BE AMAZING AT IT!

THE FACTS AND STATS

CUBA IS STILL THE ONLY COUNTRY TO HAVE EVER WON THREE OLYMPIC GOLD MEDALS IN A ROW IN VOLLEYBALL.

ON AVERAGE, DURING ONE VOLLEYBALL GAME A PLAYER CAN LEAP UP TO 300 TIMES!

MOST FEMALE VOLLEYBALL PLAYERS ARE BETWEEN 5'7" (1.7 M) AND 6'5" (1.95 M) TALL. THAT'S PRETTY TALL, BUT DON'T WORRY IF YOU'RE SHORTER THAN THAT, BECAUSE VOLLEYBALL IS ALL ABOUT SKILL AND QUICK REACTIONS.

SHORTER PLAYERS MAKE GREAT LIBEROS. BEING SHORTER HELPS THEM MAKE DIGS MORE EASILY.

THE FASTEST WOMEN'S SPIKE EVER RECORDED WAS HIT BY YANELIS SANTOS, A CUBAN PLAYER WHO SMASHED AN ASTONISHING SPIKE AT 64 MILES (103 KM) PER HOUR.

AROUND 800 MILLION PEOPLE ACROSS THE WORLD PLAY VOLLEYBALL EACH WEEK.

VOLLEYBALL WAS THE FIRST OLYMPIC TEAM SPORT THAT WOMEN COULD COMPETE IN. IT WAS INTRODUCED IN 1964 AT THE TOKYO OLYMPICS IN JAPAN.

WHEN ATTACKING, PLAYERS CAN GET REALLY HIGH IN THE AIR. FEMALE VOLLEYBALL PLAYERS HAVE BEEN RECORDED REACHING AS HIGH AS 11.9 FEET (3.39 M)!

YOUR TEAM

If volleyball sounds like the sport for you, why not give it a go? Ask all of your friends if they want to give volleyball a try.

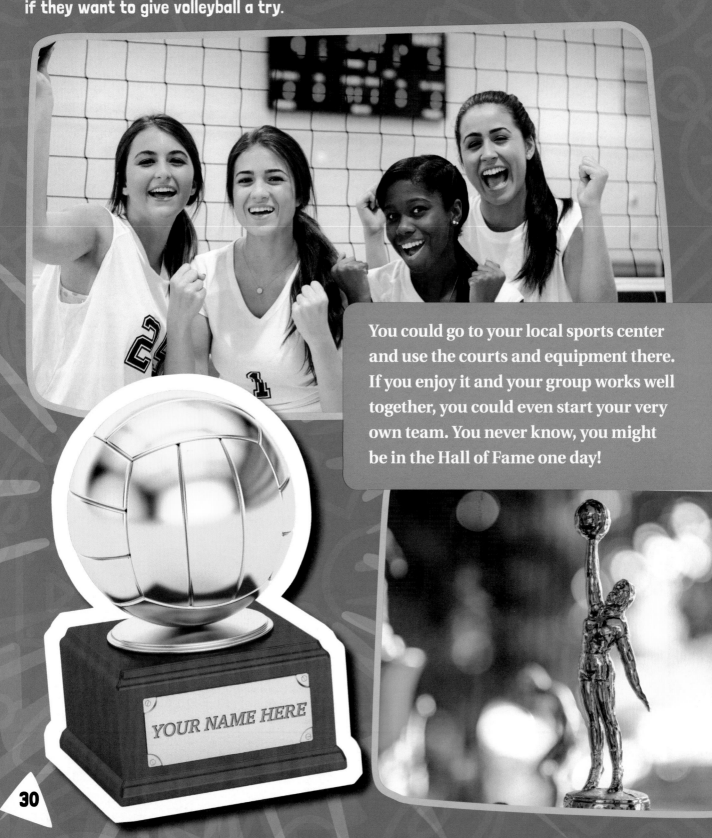

You could go to your local sports center and use the courts and equipment there. If you enjoy it and your group works well together, you could even start your very own team. You never know, you might be in the Hall of Fame one day!

YOUR NAME HERE

GLOSSARY

adaptation	a type or variation of something
amateur	someone who does something for fun rather than professionally
boundaries	the edges or limits of something
breathable	something that lets air pass through it
cardio	short for cardiovascular, a type of exercise that makes your heart do a lot of work
contact sport	a sport where players' bodies are allowed to come into contact with each other
dominant	most important or strongest
FIVB	Fédération Internationale de Volleyball, the official organization that makes decisions about professional volleyball
ligaments	a type of tissue that connects bones together or supports muscles
muscle strengthening	making your muscles stronger through exercise
opposing	on the team playing against you
optimum	the best or most desirable
preferences	what someone would rather have
prestigious	having an important and highly regarded status
professional	doing something you are good at as work
recreationally	to do something for fun rather than professionally
substitutions	people who take the place of another in a game

INDEX